Exploring
CALIFORNIA
MISSIONS

INLAND VALLEYS MISSIONS IN CALIFORNIA

❖

BY
PAULINE BROWER

❖

CONSULTANT:
JAMES J. RAWLS, PH. D.
PROFESSOR EMERITUS
DEPARTMENT OF HISTORY
DIABLO VALLEY COLLEGE

LERNER PUBLICATIONS COMPANY/MINNEAPOLIS

Photo Acknowledgments for Inland Valleys Missions

The images in this book were used with the permission of: © North Wind Picture Archives, pp. 6, 36, 48; © John Elk III, p. 8; © Eda Rogers, p. 10; © Marilyn "Angel" Wynn/Nativestock.com, p. 12; Courtesy of the Braun Research Library, Autry National Center, P. 744, p. 13; San Diego Museum of Man, p. 14; © Lake County Museum/CORBIS, p. 17; © Frank S. Balthis, pp. 18, 24, 27, 29, 32, 33, 35, 37, 38, 40, 45, 52, 54, 55, 56, 57; Zephyrin Engelhardt, The Missions and Missionaries of California, 1908-1915, pp. 21, 22, 43, 47; Courtesy of the Division of Anthropology, American Museum of Natural History (# 4051), p. 34; © Huntington Library, San Marino, CA, pp. 42, 46; Courtesy of the Bancroft Library, University of California, Berkley, p. 49; Seaver Center for Western History, Los Angeles County Museum of Natural History, p. 50.
Illustrations on pp. 4, 11, 25, 58, 59 by © Laura Westlund/Independent Picture Service.

Front cover: © Robert Holmes/CORBIS.
Back cover: © Laura Westlund/Independent Picture Service.

Lerner Publications Company
A division of Lerner Publishing Group, Inc.
241 First Avenue North
Minneapolis, MN 55401 U.S.A.

Website address: www.lernerbooks.com

Library of Congress Cataloging-in-Publication Data

Brower, Pauline.
    Inland valleys missions in California / by Pauline Brower.
        p.   cm. — (Exploring California missions)
    Includes index.
    ISBN 978-0-8225-0899-1 (lib. bdg. : alk. paper)
    1. Missions, Spanish—California—History—Juvenile literature. 2. California—History—to 1846—Juvenile literature.
3. California—History, Local—Juvenile literature. 4. Indians of North America—Missions—California—Juvenile literature.
5. Spanish mission buildings—California—Juvenile literature. I. Title.
    F862.B85 2008
    979.4—dc22   2006036847

Manufactured in the United States of America
1 2 3 4 5 6 – DP – 13 12 11 10 09 08

CONTENTS

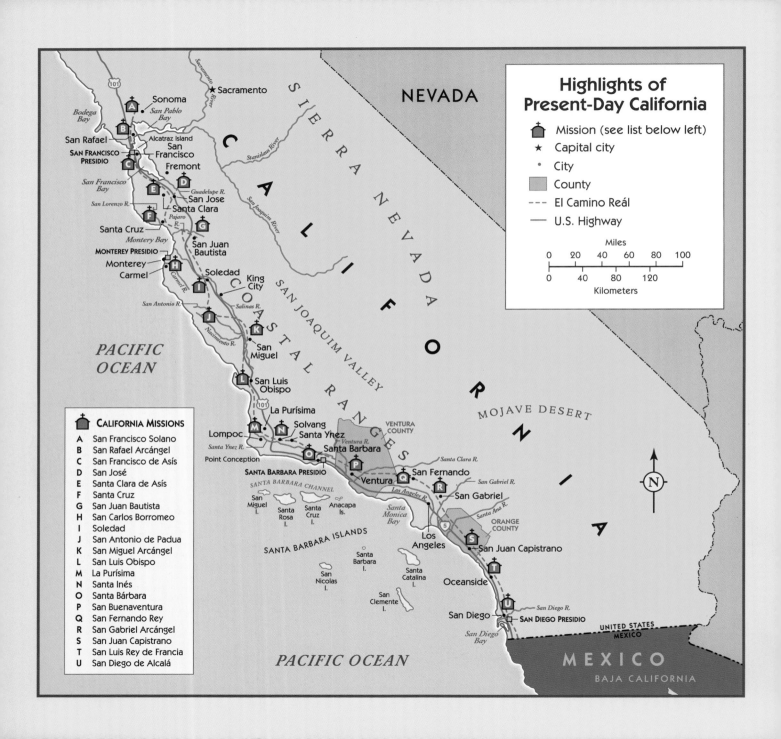

Highlights of Present-Day California

- Mission (see list below left)
- ★ Capital city
- • City
- County
- – – – El Camino Reál
- —— U.S. Highway

Miles
0 20 40 60 80 100

0 40 80 120
Kilometers

CALIFORNIA MISSIONS

A San Francisco Solano
B San Rafael Arcángel
C San Francisco de Asís
D San José
E Santa Clara de Asís
F Santa Cruz
G San Juan Bautista
H San Carlos Borromeo
I Soledad
J San Antonio de Padua
K San Miguel Arcángel
L San Luis Obispo
M La Purísima
N Santa Inés
O Santa Bárbara
P San Buenaventura
Q San Fernando Rey
R San Gabriel Arcángel
S San Juan Capistrano
T San Luis Rey de Francia
U San Diego de Alcalá

NEVADA

PACIFIC OCEAN

MEXICO
BAJA CALIFORNIA

UNITED STATES
MEXICO

MOJAVE DESERT

SIERRA NEVADA

SAN JOAQUIM VALLEY

COASTAL RANGES

CALIFORNIA

Sacramento

Sonoma
San Pablo Bay
Bodega Bay
San Rafael
SAN FRANCISCO PRESIDIO
Alcatraz Island
San Francisco
Fremont
San Francisco Bay
San Lorenzo R.
Santa Clara
San Jose
Guadalupe R.
Santa Cruz
Pajaro R.
Montery Bay
MONTEREY PRESIDIO
Monterey
Carmel
Carmel R.
San Juan Bautista
Soledad
King City
San Antonio R.
Salinas R.
Nacimiento R.
San Miguel
San Luis Obispo
La Purísima
Lompoc
Solvang
Santa Ynez
Santa Ynez R.
Point Conception
SANTA BARBARA PRESIDIO
Santa Barbara
SANTA BARBARA CHANNEL
SANTA BARBARA ISLANDS
San Miguel I.
Santa Rosa I.
Santa Cruz I.
Anacapa Is.
San Nicolas I.
Santa Barbara I.
Santa Catalina I.
San Clemente I.
Ventura
Ventura R.
VENTURA COUNTY
Santa Clara R.
San Fernando
San Gabriel R.
San Gabriel
Los Angeles R.
Los Angeles
Santa Monica Bay
Santa Ana R.
ORANGE COUNTY
San Juan Capistrano
Oceanside
San Diego R.
San Diego
San Diego Bay
SAN DIEGO PRESIDIO

Stanislaus River
San Joaquim River

PACIFIC OCEAN

INTRODUCTION

Spain and the Roman Catholic Church built twenty California **missions** between 1769 and 1817. A final mission was built in 1823. The missions stand along a narrow strip of California's Pacific coast. Today, the missions sit near Highway 101. They are between the cities of San Diego and Sonoma.

The Spaniards built **presidios** (forts) and missions throughout their empire. This system helped the Spanish claim and protect new lands. In California, the main goal of the mission system was to control Native Americans and their lands. The Spaniards wanted Native Americans to accept their leadership and way of life.

Spanish **missionaries** and soldiers ran the presidio and mission system. Father Junípero Serra was the missions' first leader. He was called father-president. Father Serra and the other priests taught Native Americans the Catholic faith. The priests showed them how to behave like Spaniards. The soldiers made sure Native Americans obeyed the priests.

The area was home to many Native American groups. They had their own beliefs and practices. The Spanish ways were much different from their own. Some Native Americans willingly joined the missions. But others did not. They did not want to give up their own ways of life.

The Spaniards tried different methods to make Native Americans join their missions. Sometimes they gave the Native Americans gifts. Other times, the Spanish used force. To stay alive, the Native Americans had no choice but to join the missions.

The Spanish called Native Americans who joined their missions **neophytes.** The Spaniards taught neophytes the Catholic religion. The neophytes built buildings and farmed the land. They also produced goods, such as cloth and soap. They built a trade route connecting the missions. It was called El Camino Reál (the Royal Road). The goods and trade were expected to earn money and power for Spain.

A Spanish missionary instructs Native Americans.

But the system did not last. More than half of the Native Americans died from diseases the Spaniards brought. Mexico took control of the area in 1821 and closed the missions. Neophytes were free to leave or stay at the missions. In 1848, the United States gained control of California. Some of the remaining neophytes returned to their people. But many others had no people to return to. They moved to **pueblos** (towns) or inland areas. The missions sat empty. They fell apart over time.

This book is about four missions built in the inland valleys of the Coast Ranges. The first of these inland valley missions was San Antonio de Padua, founded in 1771. San Luis Obispo de Tolosa was built in 1772. Nuestra Señora de la Soledad followed in 1791, and San Miguel Arcángel was founded in 1797.

CALIFORNIA MISSION	FOUNDING DATE
San Diego de Alcalá	July 16, 1769
San Carlos Borromeo de Carmelo	June 3, 1770
San Antonio de Padua	July 14, 1771
San Gabriel Arcángel	September 8, 1771
San Luis Obispo de Tolosa	September 1, 1772
San Francisco de Asís	June 29, 1776
San Juan Capistrano	November 1, 1776
Santa Clara de Asís	January 12, 1777
San Buenaventura	March 31, 1782
Santa Bárbara Virgen y Mártir	December 4, 1786
La Purísima Concepción de Maria Santísima	December 8, 1787
Santa Cruz	August 28, 1791
Nuestra Señora de la Soledad	October 9, 1791
San José	June 11, 1797
San Juan Bautista	June 24, 1797
San Miguel Arcángel	July 25, 1797
San Fernando Rey de España	September 8, 1797
San Luis Rey de Francia	June 13, 1798
Santa Inés Virgen y Mártir	September 17, 1804
San Rafael Arcángel	December 14, 1817
San Francisco Solano	July 4, 1823

Poppies are among the many wildflowers that cover California's mountain valleys in the spring.

❖1❖

EARLY LIFE IN THE INLAND VALLEYS

Near the coast in central California, the peaks of the Coast Ranges tower over broad, green inland valleys. Lakes sparkle in the sunlight. Rivers and streams make their way down the mountains to the Pacific Ocean. Summers are warm. Winters are cool. Rain is plentiful, especially in the winter and early spring.

In modern times, bustling cities sprawl across the inland valleys. But thousands of years ago, things looked very different. There were no highways or shopping malls.

Acorns from oak trees, such as this one, were an important source of food for early Native Americans in California.

Willow and oak trees, native grasses, and other plants grew freely in the rich, moist soil. Deer, elk, and antelope grazed in quiet meadows. Grizzly bears caught fish and gathered nuts and berries.

NATIVE AMERICAN LIFE

Native Americans (sometimes called American Indians) were the first people to live in California's inland valleys. But people disagree about when they first lived there. And people are not sure where Native Americans came from.

Selected
Native American
Groups in
Central and Southern
California
around 1500

N

Pomo
Lake Miwok
Patwin
Wappo
Nisenan
Coast Miwok
Miwok
Ohlone
Northern Valley Yokuts
Foothill Yokuts
Monache
Esselen
Salinan
Southern Valley Yokuts
Tubatulabal
Kitanemuk
Tataviam
Chumash
Serrano
Chumash
Tongva
Tongva (Gabrielino, Fernandeño)
Shoshonean-speakers (Luiseño, Cahuilla, Acagchemem)
Yuman-speakers (Diegueño, Kumeyaay)

Women grind acorns to make flour.

The largest groups living in the inland valleys were the Salinan and Northern Chumash Indians. Other groups included the Ohlone and the Esselen. The Yokuts lived farther east.

The Salinan and Northern Chumash rarely left their valleys. Steep cliffs, poisonous rattlesnakes, and fierce mountain lions made the mountains dangerous to cross. And people could usually find everything they needed right in the valleys. Men fished and hunted. Women and children gathered berries and cactus fruits. They also gathered pine nuts and acorns. The Native Americans ground up the acorns to make flour. They used the flour for cakes and other dishes.

The Native Americans looked to nature for more than just food. They used tree branches and long, stiff grasses to build dome-shaped homes. They made tools and weapons. They even made shampoo from the roots of the yucca plant.

When Salinan and Chumash Indians did leave the valleys, they brought along animal skins, nuts, and other items. They traded with other Native Americans for things that they did not have. Seashells were especially important. People of the inland valleys made beads from the shells and used them as money. Shells also made good tools.

Many Native Americans in California built dome-shaped homes using willow poles, reeds, and grasses.

Native Americans of the inland valleys were careful to take only what they needed from the land. They held religious ceremonies to give thanks for what Earth gave them. They believed that everything in nature was sacred —including people. They tried to treat everyone with respect.

Native American children learned from their parents. They also learned from other adults in their village. A village had spiritual leaders. They were called shamans. The village chief made decisions. He solved problems. Storytellers passed on

Some Native Americans in California used rattles made of deer hooves in religious ceremonies.

their people's beliefs. Storytellers also told of events in their history. Beginning in the mid-1500s, some of those stories must have included tales of unusual, uninvited visitors to the inland valleys. Those visitors were European explorers.

STRANGERS ARRIVE

In 1542, an explorer from Spain named Juan Rodríguez Cabrillo landed on the coast of modern-day California. The pale man didn't look like anyone the Native Americans had ever seen. Cabrillo gave them gifts of glass beads. And he gave them cloth and food. He claimed the land for Spain. Then he returned to Europe. Later, several other groups came from Spain. They wanted to explore the area. None of them stayed long.

The Spaniards called the area Alta California. *Alta* means "upper" in Spanish. The area to the south, which is modern-day western Mexico, was called Baja, or Lower, California. Together, Alta California and Baja California were known as New Spain.

In 1769, the king of Spain finally made a plan for Alta California. He wanted to settle the land. And he wanted to enlarge his empire. Captain Gaspar de Portolá and a group of soldiers set off to control and help settle the land. They set up forts called presidios. Several Franciscan priests went with them. Their leader was Junípero Serra. The priests' job was to set up Catholic missions.

As Christians, the Spaniards believed that only those who were baptized could go to heaven. Missionaries wanted to baptize as many people as they could. Those who were baptized were called neophytes. The priests expected the neophytes to leave behind their old way of life. The neophytes had to eat, dress, and worship as the Spaniards did. They also had to do most of the work at the missions. The Spaniards thought that they were teaching a better way to live.

The goal of the mission system was to spread the Catholic faith and mold the neophytes into faithful, loyal members of the Spanish Empire. The priests planned to spend ten years training and teaching the neophytes. Then the priests would leave. They would let the former neophytes run the missions

Father Junípero Serra was fifty-six years old when he founded the first California mission.

themselves. The Spaniards believed the missions would be good for everyone. The lives of the Native Americans would be improved. And the empire of Spain would be enlarged.

Captain Portolá and Father Serra had a big job to do. In July 1769, they reached modern-day San Diego. There, the Spaniards began to build California's first presidio and mission. They named the mission San Diego de Alcalá. Soon the men began to build a second presidio and mission. They were near Monterey Bay. This mission was called San Carlos Borromeo de Carmelo. Both of the missions were on the coast. This made it easy for ships to deliver supplies. But Father Serra wanted to spread the Catholic faith inland as well.

A life-size statue of Father Junípero Serra welcomes visitors to Mission San Antonio de Padua.

·2·

MISSIONS OF THE INLAND VALLEYS

Father Serra looked to the valleys of the Coast Ranges for places for his next missions. They wanted sites with good soil and plenty of water. A successful mission also needed lots of workers. The Spaniards traveled the area in search of sites. The men noticed large villages. They mapped the area. The Spaniards chose four sites for inland missions.

❖❖❖

Mission San Antonio de Padua

On July 14, 1771, Father Serra hung a bell in an oak tree. He rang it loudly. Then he raised a cross. It marked the site of the first inland mission. He named it San Antonio de Padua, after Saint Anthony of Padua, Italy. The site was near the San Antonio River. It was about seventy-five miles south of the presidio at Monterey. Two other priests, several soldiers, and two neophyte families were also there. These people would be the first to live at the mission.

Curious Salinan Indians heard the bell and gathered to watch. The priests welcomed them with gifts. Soon the whole group began to build a wooden church and some basic shelters.

Father Serra left priests Buenaventura Sitjar and Miguel Pieras in charge. Right away, the men began to learn the Salinan language. They also offered the Salinan people beads, glass, and cloth. The gifts convinced some of the area people to join the mission. They were baptized by the priests.

A priest baptizes a Native American baby. This ceremony welcomed the baby into the Catholic Church.

Once baptized, a neophyte had to live at the mission. The priests set up a strict schedule of work, meals, and religious study. The day started at sunrise. It began with a breakfast of *atole*, a porridge made from corn. Sometimes food was scarce. This was especially true in the mission's first year. After breakfast, everyone gathered for prayers. Then they headed to their jobs.

Almost everything the mission needed had to be made or grown there. The neophytes did most of the work. The men worked in the fields. They grew crops of wheat, corn, and beans. They also tended livestock, fruit trees, and grapevines. Some made iron or leather goods. Many of the women cooked meals. They also wove cloth, sewed clothing, and made candles.

At the missions, neophytes farmed the land.

The neophytes took a break for lunch. It was often a stew called posole. Then they returned to work. They worked until dinnertime. The evening meal was followed by another church service. Only after the service could they relax.

Some neophytes liked this new life. Others longed to return to their villages. But the Spaniards would not let the neophytes leave. If they tried to run away, they were beaten. Sometimes they were locked up. The priests needed them to make the mission a success.

In 1773, a lack of rain forced the priests at San Antonio to move the mission a short distance upriver. More water was at the new site. The neophytes built storage rooms, workshops, kitchens, a church, and sleeping quarters. The buildings were laid out in a rectangle. They stood around an open courtyard. This arrangement was called a **quadrangle.**

The structures at the new site were built of bricks made of **adobe.** Neophytes made each brick. First, they mixed together clay, mud, and water. They packed the mixture into rectangular molds. The bricks dried in the sun. Then the workers covered them with plaster. That made them more waterproof.

Workers made hundreds of bricks each day. They had to keep up with the demand for new buildings. In its first two years, the mission had been slow to attract neophytes. But by 1773, priests had baptized 158 people. Each person needed room to sleep, eat, work, and pray.

One of the biggest jobs the neophytes faced was hauling water from the river. The mission needed water for drinking, cooking, cleaning, and farming. The priests at San Antonio designed a system of stone ditches. They were called aqueducts. The aqueducts carried water from the river to the mission. San Antonio grew. So did its system of aqueducts.

Neophytes used rectangular molds to make adobe bricks.

How a Mission Looked

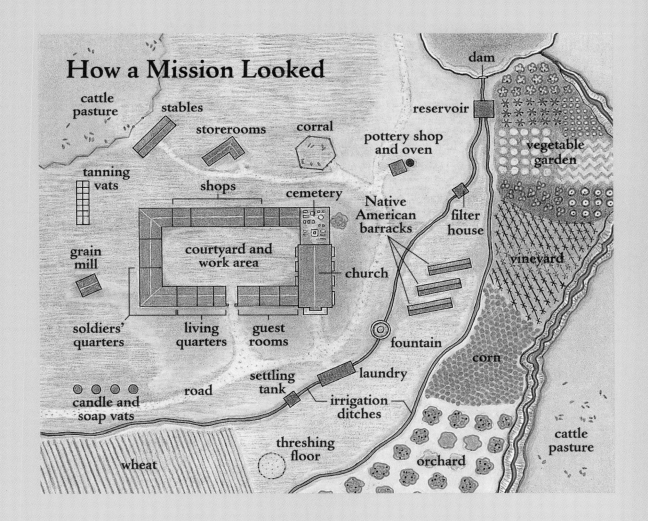

cattle pasture

stables

storerooms

corral

pottery shop and oven

dam

reservoir

vegetable garden

tanning vats

shops

cemetery

Native American barracks

filter house

vineyard

grain mill

courtyard and work area

church

soldiers' quarters

living quarters

guest rooms

fountain

corn

candle and soap vats

road

settling tank

laundry

irrigation ditches

cattle pasture

wheat

threshing floor

orchard

Over the years, neophytes built miles of aqueducts. They also built large pools. The pools stored water for times when the river was low.

Mission San Antonio grew and flourished. More and more land was claimed for wheat fields, vineyards, and orchards. The crops that the mission did not need were sold. Or they were traded to other missions. By 1810, the population of San Antonio had grown to thirteen hundred. The mission cared for seventeen thousand cattle and sheep. The mission was well known for its strong horses and tart wine.

That same year, neophytes began a major building project. The mission needed a new church to hold its growing population. It took three years to finish. The beautiful building had high ceilings. It was a source of pride at the mission for years.

❖❖❖

MISSION SAN LUIS OBISPO DE TOLOSA

On September 1, 1772, Father Serra blessed the site for Mission San Luis Obispo de Tolosa. It was named after a

A statue of a bear rests outside the church at Mission San Luis Obispo. The statue honors the many grizzlies that once roamed the area.

bishop from Toulouse, France. This new mission was in an area the Spaniards called the Valley de los Osos (of the Bears). It was known for its good hunting. It also seemed to have plenty of water, mild weather, and friendly neighbors. Father Serra chose Father José Cavaller to run San Luis Obispo. He also assigned five soldiers and two neophytes to the mission.

The Northern Chumash Indians lived nearby. At first, mission life was not attractive to them. Even in the Valley of the Bears, there wasn't always enough food at the mission.

The priests' strict schedule left little time for play or rest. Still, friendly neighbors were willing to help with the mission's construction. Some people even brought their children to be baptized. A few Chumash did join the mission.

This new life was not easy for the neophytes. As at the other missions, soldiers beat them if they did not follow the rules. They could not practice their own religions. They worked hard all day long. But they received no pay. To keep the neophytes happy, the priests sometimes allowed them to hold traditional ceremonies. They sang and danced to their own music. Still, many neophytes did not like being told how to live.

Early harvests at San Luis Obispo were better than expected. The promise of a steady food supply attracted more Chumash. The mission flourished. Workers built strong wooden buildings. They made roofs of stiff, dried grasses. They began to make goods and supplies.

But some Native Americans in the area were unhappy. They didn't like to see the mission doing well. The Spaniards had settled on their prized hunting grounds.

The American Indians wanted the Spaniards to leave. They shot burning arrows into the roofs of mission buildings. More attacks followed. By 1776, all but two of the buildings had burned down.

The Spaniards did not give up. They rebuilt the mission. This time, workers used adobe bricks for the walls. Adobe would not catch fire. However, it could be damaged by wet weather. An adobe building needed a good roof. The priest decided that tile roofs, like those in Spain, would be perfect.

Mission San Luis Obispo was the first to use fireproof tiles on its roof.

He showed the neophytes how to lay strips of clay over tree limbs to dry. Next the workers baked the clay in an oven. The hard, curved tiles stopped burning arrows. Soon the other missions began to use them too. The tiles also kept the adobe buildings dry.

The quadrangle at San Luis Obispo included storerooms, workshops, and mills. It also had living quarters for the neophytes. As at all the missions, unmarried women and girls were locked in their rooms at night. Men and boys were not locked up. In 1794, the mission added a church and priests' quarters.

In 1798, Father Luís Antonio Martínez joined San Luis Obispo. He was a friendly man. He got along well with the Chumash Indians. He showed the neophytes how to grow olives, grapes, and other fruit. The workers built houses for families. They also built a storehouse for grain and a weaving room. The mission also added two ranchos, or ranches. They were set apart from the main mission grounds. The ranchos were used to raise cattle and other livestock.

By 1803, San Luis Obispo had 961 neophytes. The mission supported itself in a number of ways. The neophytes made and sold olive oil and wine. They made leather goods, such as shoes and saddles. The mission still had plenty left over to provide for its own people.

MISSION NUESTRA SEÑORA DE LA SOLEDAD

Father Serra was busy. Between 1776 and 1782, he founded four more missions in California. That made nine in all. Then, in 1784, Father Serra died. Father Fermín Francisco de Lasuén took over as head of the mission system. Like Father Serra, Father Lasuén was determined to spread his faith. In his first three years on the job, he founded two missions on the coast. Then, once again, the focus turned inland.

During Captain Portolá's 1769 expedition, he noticed a promising inland site south of Monterey. The site was in a wide valley. It was halfway between Monterey and Mission San Antonio. A mission on this site would be useful.

Mission Nuestra Señora de la Soledad had a difficult beginning.

It would give travelers a place to stop and rest. On October 9, 1791, Father Lasuén founded Mission Nuestra Señora de la Soledad. The name means "Our Lady of Solitude." The lady is Mary, the mother of Jesus.

California's thirteenth mission quickly ran into trouble. The weather was the biggest problem. Winters in the valley

From the time of its founding, Soledad was a troubled and lonely mission

were damp and cold. Summers were harsh and hot. Crops did poorly. People at the mission were often sick and hungry. Priests who came to the mission soon asked to leave.

In the first year, priests baptized only eleven Salinan Indians. With so few hands, little work got done. Workers completed an adobe church in 1797. But the mission saw more struggles than successes. In its first eight years, the Salinas River flooded three times. Several earthquakes shook the area. Each disaster caused damage to the mission.

Despite its hardships, the mission slowly grew. Five hundred neophytes lived and worked at the mission by 1800. They worked in the fields, made goods, and tended three thousand cattle and sheep.

Then, in 1802, a terrible disease spread through the mission. For a time, several neophytes died every day. Others ran away. They were afraid they would get sick. Disease was a big problem at the other missions too. The Spaniards brought illnesses from Europe. They were new to the Native Americans. Their bodies could not fight the diseases. Thousands of neophytes died.

In 1803, a new priest came to run Soledad. Father

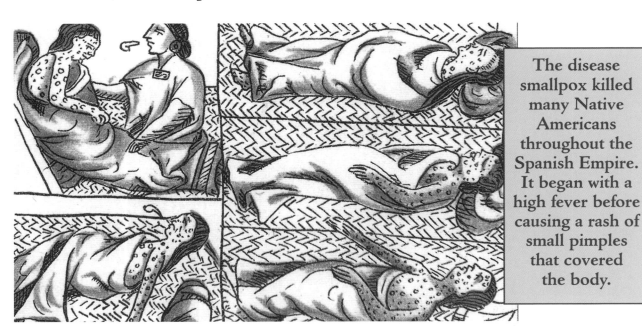

The disease smallpox killed many Native Americans throughout the Spanish Empire. It began with a high fever before causing a rash of small pimples that covered the body.

Colorful paintings still adorn the walls of Mission San Miguel Arcángel.

Florencio Ibáñez was a good teacher and a good businessman. He set up a strict schedule for the neophytes. In the mornings, he led them in prayers and religion classes. The priest believed this was his most important job. Breakfast followed. Then the neophytes headed to their day's work. In the evenings, Father Ibañez encouraged the neophytes to relax. They sang and played music. And they acted out plays.

Within two years, the population at Mission Soledad grew to 688. Still, the mission struggled. Few Native Americans lived nearby. And visitors rarely came. Some people called Soledad "the Forgotten Mission."

❖❖❖

MISSION SAN MIGUEL ARCÁNGEL

Father Lasuén founded San Miguel Arcángel the last inland valley mission on July 25, 1797.

Priests, Spanish soldiers, and Native Americans gathered together at the California missions.

It was named for the archangel (chief angel) Michael. At San Miguel's first Mass, or church service, priests baptized fifteen Salinan children. A large group of Salinan Indians lived close by. Father Lasuén saw this as a sign that the mission would succeed.

Two rivers, the Salinas and the Nacimiento, joined near the mission site. The area was good for raising crops and livestock. The first priests to lead Mission San Miguel were Buenaventura Sitjar and Antonio de la Concepción Horra. Father Horra left after only two months. He told leaders of the

Candles glimmer at a side altar of the church in San Miguel.

Catholic Church that Father Sitjar had treated the neophytes badly. He claimed that Father Sitjar had neophytes beaten, chained up, or locked away without food or water. The Church didn't believe Father Horra's stories. But many historians think the priest was telling the truth.

Eventually Father Lasuén sent two other priests, Juan Martín and Juan Cabot, to run the mission. The priests reached out to their Salinan neighbors. In their first year, they baptized 185 neophytes. A successful harvest brought in huge crops. The mission grew wheat, barley, corn, peas, and beans. The mission was able to grow and make almost everything it needed.

After eight years, San Miguel was home to 949 neophytes. Adobe buildings lined the quadrangle. But in 1806, a terrible fire swept through the mission. Buildings and supplies were destroyed. The biggest loss was the church. It burned to the ground.

After the fire, the priests decided to build a bigger and better church. It took twelve years. By this time, San Miguel covered hundreds of acres. About two thousand neophytes lived there. They tended about twelve thousand animals. But the mission isn't remembered for its size.

This gate marks the entrance to the cemetery at San Miguel.

In 1821, a Spanish artist named Estéban Munras came to the mission. He taught the neophytes how to make paintings called **frescoes** on the walls of the new church. First the artists spread new plaster on a small part of a wall. Then they painted the area with bright colors. They had to work quickly to finish before the plaster dried. A fresco painting became part of the wall itself. The neophytes at San Miguel were talented artists. Visitors came just to see its beautiful church.

An old adobe wall frames this vineyard at
Mission Nuestra Señora de la Soledad.

STATE CONTROL OF THE MISSIONS

During the early 1800s, Spain began to have trouble controlling New Spain and other parts of its empire. New settlers had come to live in territories such as California. They built ranchos. They also lived in pueblos. They saw that the missions were running smoothly. They wanted the missions' valuable land for themselves. They also wanted to be free from Spain's unfair laws.

The Californios wanted land that was proven to be good for farming and ranching.

In 1810, the people of New Spain went to war against Spain. In 1821, the people won their freedom. They gave their country a new name, the Republic of Mexico. They also claimed Alta California and its valuable missions.

In 1833, the Mexican government began to pass laws to **secularize** the missions. These laws took control of mission lands away from the Spanish priests. The laws set out plans for dividing and selling the mission lands. The Mexican government hired administrators to carry out the plans. The administrators were supposed to make sure that the land was divided fairly. Some property was to be given to neophytes. But few neophytes ever received any of the mission lands.

The Mexican government gave land to **Californios.** The Californios were settlers and ranchers who had come from Mexico to live in California. The Mexican government saw the Californios as Mexican citizens. By giving land in California to its own citizens, Mexico strengthened its claim to the territory.

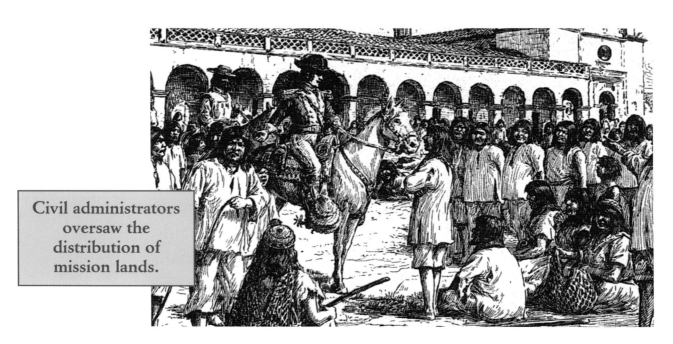

Civil administrators oversaw the distribution of mission lands.

THE MISSIONS CLOSE THEIR DOORS

Mexico began to secularize the missions in 1833. Most of them were already failing. Mission San Antonio was the first inland valley mission to be secularized. The Mexican government took control from the priests in 1834. Most of the neophytes left. No one was left to care for the mission. Its buildings fell down.

In 1835, the government secularized San Luis Obispo. Only a small group of neophytes lived there. And they were seriously ill. Much of the mission's livestock had been stolen.

Mission Soledad was already falling apart when it was secularized in 1835. The priest had died. Almost all the neophytes had left.

San Miguel was still a successful ranch and vineyard. Mexican officials came to take control of the mission in 1836. The Mexicans treated the Salinan workers harshly. Many of them left. Without the Salinan neophytes, the officials couldn't keep up with the work. Like the other missions, San Miguel also failed.

The olive press is one of the many tools that was used at the old Mission San Miguel.

NATIVE AMERICANS

After secularization, the neophytes were free to leave the missions. Most of these Native Americans were happy to be free. But many neophytes had nowhere to go. Their villages had been wiped out by disease. Their people had been forced off their lands by missions or ranchers.

It was difficult for the neophytes to make a living. Most of them had grown up at the missions. They didn't know how to live off the land, as their ancestors had. Some received land from the government. They became farmers. But often, the Californios tricked Native American landowners into selling their land at cheap prices. Many neophytes found low-paying jobs in pueblos. Others worked on ranchos. For their labor, they usually received nothing more than shelter, food, and clothing.

MISSIONS FOR SALE

In the mid-1840s, the Mexican government still owned some of the mission lands. In 1845, an administrator named Pío Pico became governor of California. He sold what was left of the missions, including San Luis Obispo, Soledad, and San Miguel. In July 1846, just three days after the sale of San Miguel, the U.S. Marines attacked at Monterey Bay.

Governor Pío Pico sold or gave away mission land to his friends and relatives.

THE UNITED STATES TAKES OVER

For several years, the United States and Mexico had argued over the countries' borders. They disagreed over the boundary between Mexico and the state of Texas. The United States also wanted California. In 1846, the United States decided to go to war. Mexico couldn't afford to send large armies to California. In less than two years, the Mexican War was over. Mexico gave up about half of its lands. On September 9, 1850, the United States made California its thirty-first state.

Throughout the war, the U.S. flag flew over Monterey Bay.

About this same time, miners discovered gold in California. People came from all over the world. They hoped to strike it rich. They all wanted to own property in California.

Californios had to prove that they owned their land. Some couldn't show proof. Then the U.S. government took the land away. The government sold the land to other U.S. citizens instead.

The U.S. government didn't think Native Americans had the right to own land. Even those who could prove their ownership lost their land. Instead, the government set aside areas called **reservations** for the

Prospectors came to California in search of the gold found in streams and mines.

Many Native Americans in California were forced by the government to give up their land.

Native Americans. These lands often had little value. The soil was poor, and there was little wildlife for hunting. People on the reservations had to depend on the government for food. The California Indians struggled to keep alive their old ways of life.

In the late 1800s, the mission paintings of British artist Edwin Deakin sparked people's interest in restoring the decaying buildings. By this time, little remained of Nuestra Señora de la Soledad.

·4·

THE MISSIONS IN MODERN TIMES

After secularization, the missions were almost forgotten. By 1865, the United States had returned all twenty-one mission sites to the Catholic Church. But the church had no money to rebuild them. Then, in 1902, a group of history lovers started the California Historic Landmarks League. They wanted to raise money to **restore** the missions and other historic sites. Rebuilding these sites would allow people to learn about early California history.

The restored church at Mission San Antonio looks like the original building.

SAN ANTONIO

Mission San Antonio was the Landmarks League's first project in the inland valleys. The work began in 1903. But heavy rains and a terrible earthquake damaged some of the restored buildings. Work continued until the project ran out of money in 1907.

By 1948, even areas that had been rebuilt had been damaged by wind and rain. Catholic priests made plans to rebuild again. A group called the Hearst Foundation gave them money for the project. This time, workers hid concrete and steel in the adobe walls. That made them stronger. When the work was done, Mission San Antonio looked just as it did two hundred years ago. Even the land around it remains as it once was.

SAN LUIS OBISPO

In the years after secularization, San Luis Obispo went through many changes. In the mid-1800s, the bustling town of San Luis Obispo grew up around the mission. By 1868, the church's adobe walls and tile roof were crumbling. Townspeople covered the walls with wood. They replaced the roof tiles with wooden shingles. They also added a bell tower.

In 1920, a fire destroyed the wooden roof. But the original ceiling underneath did not burn. The neophytes' hand-painted designs remained. Some church members made plans to restore the building. They did research. They wanted to find out what it looked like when it was first built.

In 1933, workers rebuilt the church's adobe walls. They also added a tile roof. They restored a few other mission buildings as well. There wasn't room to rebuild the whole quadrangle. Newer buildings stood in the way.

A statue of Father Junípera Serra stands in the courtyard of Mission San Luis Obispo.

The original bell stands near the entrance to the church at Mission Nuestra Señora de la Soledad

SOLEDAD

In 1832, a flood at Mission Soledad had washed away most of the remaining buildings. Little was left to be restored. Finally, in 1954, a local group rebuilt the mission church. Later, they restored the living quarters. But the group did not have enough money to continue. The church, gardens, and a museum are open to the public.

A fountain stands in the center of the courtyard at Mission San Miguel Arcángel. In the old mission days, a fountain was important in a dry environment.

SAN MIGUEL

Like the other missions, San Miguel slowly fell apart after secularization. Priests made repairs to the church in 1878. This allowed them to hold services there.

Fifty years later, the Catholic Church returned the mission to the Franciscans. The priests completely restored the mission. They planted new trees where others had once stood. But they did no work on the famous frescoes. Visitors to San Miguel can still admire the neophytes' beautiful work.

MODERN-DAY INLAND VALLEY MISSIONS

All four of the inland valley missions are open to visitors. Some, such as San Antonio, are fully restored. Other sites, such as Soledad, simply offer a glimpse into their past. People can tour the restored buildings. Tourists can picnic under ancient oak trees. They can also attend religious services. Museums use artwork and everyday items to show what mission life was like.

This photo shows one corner of the old kitchen at Mission San Antonio de Padua.

More than two hundred years have passed since Spaniards planted the first mission cross in California. Spanish culture can still be seen in the place names and building styles. The influence of the Native Americans can also be seen. They have overcome great hardships. The towns and cities in the area have become home to a new way of life.

LAYOUTS

These diagrams of California's inland valley missions show what the missions look like in modern times. Modern-day missions may not look exactly like the original missions Spanish priests founded. But by studying them, we can get a sense of how neophytes and missionaries lived.

San Luis Obispo:
For the site of San Luis Obispo de Tolosa, Father Serra chose an area inhabited by the Chumash. The fifth California mission, San Luis Obispo was founded in 1772.

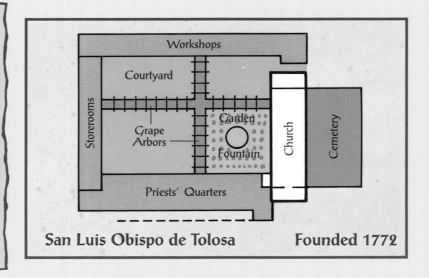

Workshops

Courtyard

Storerooms

Grape Arbors

Garden

Fountain

Church

Cemetery

Priests' Quarters

San Luis Obispo de Tolosa   Founded 1772

Nuestra Señora de la Soledad:

A troubled mission from its founding, Nuestra Señora de la Soledad was built in 1791 in a valley that an early expedition mistook for Monterey Bay.

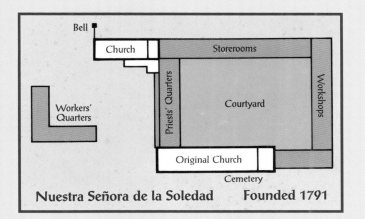

Nuestra Señora de la Soledad   Founded 1791

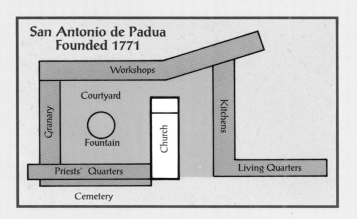

San Miguel Arcángel:

Situated near the joining of the Salinas and Nacimiento Rivers, Mission San Miguel Arcángel was successful from its founding in 1797.

San Antonio de Padua:

Mission San Antonio de Padua, set up in 1771 near the San Antonio River, was rebuilt a short distance from San Miguel Creek after the river dried up.

TIMELINE

1769   Padre Junípero Serra blesses the site of the first mission

1771   San Antonio de Padua becomes the first inland mission

1772   Padre Serra founds Mission San Luis Obispo

1784   Padre Serra dies. Padre Fermín Francisco de Lasuén takes over as father president of the mission system

1791   Padre Lasuén blesses the site of Mission Nuestra Señora de la Soledad.

1797   Mission San Miguel Arcángel is founded

1810   The people of New Spain go to war against Spain

1821   New Spain wins its independence and becomes the Republic of Mexico

1830s   Missions are secularized. Mission buildings begin to crumble

1846   The Mexican War begins

1848   Mexico loses the war and gives California to the United States

1850   California becomes the thirty-first state

1850s   The U.S. government returns the missions to the Catholic Church

1890s–   Mission restoration begins and continues to present time

GLOSSARY

adobe: a mixture of clay, straw, and water that is formed into bricks and baked in the sun. Adobe walls kept buildings cool in the summer and warm in the winter.

Californios: settlers from Spain and other areas of New Spain who made their homes in California

frescoes: artwork made by painting on wet plaster walls. Fresco paintings decorate the walls of many mission churches.

missionaries: Christians who work to spread their faith to people of other religions

missions: centers where religious people teach others about the Christian faith

neophytes: the name given to Native Americans who were baptized into the Catholic Church

presidios: Spanish military forts. The forts protected the missions and enforced Spanish laws in California.

pueblos: the Spanish word for towns

quadrangle: a rectangular arrangement of buildings with an open courtyard in the middle

reservations: lands reserved, or set aside, for Native Americans

restore: to bring something back to its original appearance

secularize: to take control of the mission lands from the Spanish priests. The missions were secularized when the Mexican government gave the lands to other settlers.

PRONUNCIATION GUIDE*

Chumash	CHOO-mash
El Camino Reál	el kah-MEE-no ray-AHL
Esselen	EHS-suh-luhn
Ibáñez, Florencio	ee-BAHN-yehs, floh-REHN-see-oh
Lasuén, Fermín Francisco de	lah-soo-AYN, fair-MEEN frahn-SEES-koh day
Nuestra Señora de la Soledad	noo-EHS-trah sehn-YOH-rah day lah soh-lay-DAHD
Ohlone	oh-LOH-nee
Portolá, Gaspar de	por-toh-LAH, gahs-PAHR day
Salinan	Suh-LEE-nuhn
San Antonia de Padua	SAHN ahn-TOH-nee-oh day PAH-d'wah
San Luis Obispo de Tolosa	SAHN loo-EES oh-BEES-poh day toh-LOH-sah
San Miguel Arcángel	SAHN mee-GAYL ahr-KAHN-hayl
Serra, Junípero	SHE-rrah, hoo-NEE-pay-roh
Yokuts	YOH-kuhts

*Local pronunciations may differ.

TO LEARN MORE

Behrens, June. *Central Coast Missions in California.* Minneapolis: Lerner Publications Company, 2008. Learn about the missions of California's central coast.

Mission Nuestra Señora de la Soledad
http://www.missionart.com/hSOL/p-SOL.html
Take a photo tour of the California missions, starting in Soledad.

Nelson, Libby, and Kari A. Cornell. *California Mission Projects and Layouts.* Minneapolis: Lerner Publications Company, 2008. This book provides guides on how to build a mission model.

San Antonio de Padua
http://www.athanasius.com/camission/padua.htm
Learn what life was like at this mission.

San Luis Obispo de Tolosa
http://www.athanasius.com/camission/obispo.htm
Learn about this mission's many changes.

San Miguel Arcángel.
http://www.athanasius.com/camission/miguel.htm
Learn all about Mission San Miguel Arcángel and view color photographs.

Sonneborn, Liz. *The Chumash.* Minneapolis: Lerner Publications Company, 2007. This book introduces the Chumash, Native Americans whose homeland is in California.

Van Steenwyk, Elizabeth. *The California Missions.* New York: Franklin Watts, 1995. Van Steenwyk introduces California missions through clear text and full-color photographs.

INDEX